This library edition published in 2011 by Walter Foster Publishing, Inc.
Walter Foster Library
Distributed by Black Rabbit Books.
P.O. Box 3263 Mankato, Minnesota 56002

Printed in China, Shanghai Offset Printing Products Limited, Shenzhen.

First Library Edition

Library of Congress Cataloging-in-Publication Data

Baggetta, Marla.
  Pastel step by step / by Marla Baggetta. -- 1st library ed.
    p. cm. -- (Artist's library series)
  ISBN 978-1-936309-25-2 (hardcover)
  1. Pastel drawing--Technique. I. Title.
  NC880.B34 2011
  741.2'35--dc22
                                                            2010005937

032010
0P1815

9 8 7 6 5 4 3 2 1

Pastel
Step by Step

by Marla Baggetta

www.walterfoster.com

Contents

Introduction

If you like working with color, then you'll love pastels! Pastel has recently experienced a renewed popularity as a serious painting medium, and several manufacturers now make high-quality materials readily available to artists. Pastels are easy to use, and you don't have to worry about drying times, toxicity, or odors—as you might if you were working with paint. And pastel is also attractive to many artists because of its versatility—it is both a painting and a drawing medium. Moreover, you can create a seemingly endless variety of textures and effects with the vast number of hues that are available. And pastel is an extremely fluid and forgiving medium, which makes it great for beginners.

I've tried many other media throughout the years, but I always seem to come back to pastel. It is now my medium of choice, and I work almost exclusively in soft pastel. In this book, I'll demonstrate a variety of techniques and show you how to render an array of subject matter—we'll even explore working with different artistic styles. As you learn more about the vibrant and fascinating world of pastel, you'll begin to recognize the endless possibilities that this medium has to offer!

Although you won't need a lot of supplies to work in pastel, you will want a large assortment of colors. You can't mix pastel colors on a palette (as you would with paint) before applying them to the support—you must layer and blend them directly on the paper itself. But pastels are available in thousands of colors, and since they never "expire," you can buy as many colors as you like and keep them indefinitely. Most pastel manufacturers offer sets that contain a variety of colors and values. (For more on values, see page 6.) If you're a beginner, buying sets is a good way to start building your collection; you can always purchase additional individual pastels later. For the projects in this book, I've listed the colors I use at the beginning of each lesson. Of course you can substitute similar colors, but your results may differ from mine.

Pastels

There are two styles of pastel available: chalk-based pastels and oil pastels. In this book, I use a combination of the three types of chalk-based pastel—hard, clay-based sticks; soft pastel sticks; and pastel pencils. Hard pastels are good for underpainting (see page 12) and filling in large areas, while the buttery consistency of soft pastels makes them ideal for soft blends and smooth textures. Pastel pencils provide precise control and brilliant color, making them a good choice for detail work.

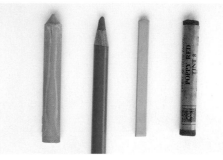

Choosing Pastels Remember that it's important to buy the best quality of materials that you can afford: Artist-grade pastels contain more pigment and less binder than the inexpensive student-grade ones, making artist-grade more vibrant and less likely to crumble.

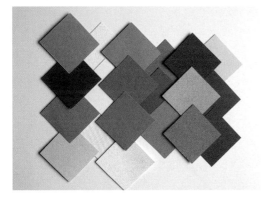

Choosing a Support Don't let the staggering array of available supports overwhelm you; you can limit your selection somewhat by sticking to archival-quality papers, which are specially treated to retain the brilliance of the pigment you apply. This way your work will remain as vibrant as when you first created it.

Supports

The paper you work on—your *support*—contributes greatly to the effects you achieve. There are three important aspects to consider when you're choosing a support: The *tooth* (or the grain), the tone, and the color. The tooth can be rough or smooth; the tone can be dark or light; and the color can be cool, warm, or neutral. (For more on color, see pages 6–7.) Rough papers are best for thick layers of pigment, while smooth papers have less tooth, so they are better for soft blends and detail work. The tone and the color of the support you choose will affect the mood of your subject; cool, dark papers can evoke a dramatic feeling, while lighter, warmer papers may create a more lighthearted feeling.

Organizing Pastels When I paint, I arrange my pastels on a plywood tray I built myself. I lined each section with foam to help keep the pastels clean and to prevent them from rolling around and breaking. I also have room on my tray for my other tools, as well as space for expansion—I'm always collecting new colors!

Sharpening Tools To sharpen soft pastel sticks, I use a sandpaper pad or a drywall screen. When sharpening hard pastel sticks, I prefer using a utility knife. Most pastel pencils can be sharpened with a small hand-held pencil sharpener or an electric sharpener.

Setting Up a Workspace My workspace is arranged so that everything I need is nearby and easily accessible. I set up my easel with a trap underneath to collect any excess pastel dust. My support is fairly vertical—this way, the pastel dust will fall into the trap instead of onto the floor. For health and safety reasons, I always keep my workspace well ventilated so I don't breathe in the pastel dust.

Painting Outdoors

Painting outdoors, or *en plein air,* is a great way to observe your subject. And pastels are perfect for painting on site—they are easy to transport and there's virtually no cleanup involved. When I paint outdoors, I use a French easel (also called a "pochade") with a custom-made tray that accommodates all my pastels. When setting up, I usually face my easel toward the sun so the shadow of my easel shields my pastels and keeps my working surface shaded. When traveling or painting outdoors, I keep my pastels in tight-lidded plastic containers filled with cornmeal. This system not only keeps the pastels clean, but also assures they will stay unbroken during transport.

Bringing the Essentials There are a few extra items you might want to bring with you when you paint outdoors. It's always a good idea to have a hat and sunscreen, even on cloudy days, along with plenty of water, snacks, bug spray, a poncho in case it rains, and a charged cell phone. And don't forget handwarmers and a thermos of a warm beverage on cold days!

Color Theory

Since pastels are blended directly on the support, it's important to know the basics of color theory; this way, you can learn to mix color accurately. The *primary* colors (red, yellow, and blue) are the three basic colors that can't be created by mixing other colors; all other colors are derived from these three. The *secondary* colors (orange, green, and purple) are each a combination of two primaries, and the *tertiary* colors (red-orange, red-purple, yellow-orange, yellow-green, blue-green, and blue-purple) are each a combination of a primary color and a secondary color. Each color is referred to by its *hue,* or name, (such as green or blue) and its *saturation* or intensity (its relative brightness or dullness).

Color Wheel Knowing where each color lies on the color wheel will help you understand how colors relate and interact with one another; it will also help you understand how to mix and blend your own pastel hues.

Using Complements *Complementary* colors are any two colors directly across from each other on the color wheel (such as red and green, orange and blue, or yellow and purple). When placed next to each other, complementary colors can create lively contrasts in your artwork. When blended, they neutralize each other, creating fresh grays and browns.

Value

Value refers to the relative lightness or darkness of a color—or black. Effectively manipulating value creates the illusion of form in a painting. The concept of value is especially important when working with pastel, as pastel manufacturers produce each hue in a variety of values, from light to dark. They label their pastels using a numbering system to identify

Making a Value Scale A value scale starts with a dark value of a color (or black), progresses through values of gray which gradually become lighter, and finally becomes almost white. This value scale demonstrates the value progression of black to white. Creating a value scale like this will be a helpful reference tool as you paint; refer to it often to help you see the variations of value in your subjects.

the strength of each color. (For example, one manufacturer labels the pure color as "5," with the lightest value being "1" and the darkest "9." Another brand uses decimal points to denote the proportion of white that has been added to the pure hue.) Unfortunately these numbering systems are not standardized among brands. When you purchase pastels, compare the labels carefully to determine how that particular manufacturer indicates the values of its colors.

Tints, Shades, and Tones

When pastel manufacturers create various values of the same color, they add white to make it lighter, creating a *tint*, or they add black to make it darker, creating a *shade*. To mute a color, gray is added, creating a *tone*. You can expand your pastel palette by purchasing a variety of tints, shades, and tones from the manufacturer, or you can experiment with creating your own mixtures by blending white, black, or gray into your colors.

Creating Tints and Shades In this example, the pure color is in the middle of each bar. Black was blended in at the left and white at the right. When creating your own tints and shades, keep the layers of color light so that you don't fill the tooth of the paper; that way it will still be able to hold more pigment.

Color Psychology

Colors are often referred to in terms of "temperature," but that doesn't mean actual heat. An easy way to understand color temperature is to think of the color wheel as divided into two halves: The colors on the red side (red, orange, and yellow) are considered *warm*, while the colors on the blue side (blue, green, and purple) are considered *cool*. Thus colors with red or yellow in them also appear warmer, and colors with more green or blue in them appear cooler. For instance, if a normally cool color (like green) has more yellow added to it, it will appear warmer; and if a normally warm color (like red) has a little blue, it will seem cooler. Another important point to remember about color temperature is that warm colors appear to come forward and cool colors appear to recede; this knowledge is valuable when creating the illusion of depth in a scene. (See pages 22–25 for a demonstration of this principle in a pastel landscape.)

Comparing Warm and Cool Here the same scene is drawn with two different palettes; one warm (left) and one cool (right). Notice that the mood is strikingly different in each scene. This is because color arouses certain feelings; for example, warm colors generally convey energy and excitement, whereas cooler colors usually indicate peace and calm.

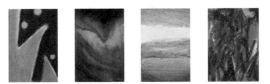

Expressing Mood The examples above further illustrate how color can be used to create mood (left to right): Complements can create a sense of tension; cool hues can evoke a sense of mystery; light, cool colors can provide a feeling of tranquility; and warm colors can impart a sense of danger.

Unlike painting with a brush, working with pastel allows you to make direct contact with the support. Therefore you have much more control over the strokes you make, the way you blend the pigment, and the final effects. Once you learn and practice the techniques shown here, you'll know which ones will give you the results you desire.

Firm Strokes Use the ends of the pastel sticks to create thick, bold strokes. The more pressure you apply, the thicker the stroke will be. These strokes are ideal for rendering large textured areas, such as fields of grass .

Side Strokes To quickly cover the support and fill in areas of broad color, drag the side of the stick across the support. I use this technique frequently to create skies, water, and under-paintings.

Pencil Lines Pastel pencils offer the most line control, as they are less likely to crumble or break than other types of pastel. If sharp, they can produce a very fine line, which is ideal for creating details or textures, such as fur or hair.

Handling Pastels

The way you hold and manipulate the pastel stick or pencil will directly affect the resulting stroke. Some grips will give you more control than others, making them better for detail work, and some will allow you to apply more pigment to the support to create broad coverage. And the pressure you exert will affect the intensity of the color and the weight of the line you create. Experiment with each of the grips described below to discover which are most comfortable and effective for you.

Linear Strokes To create linear strokes, grip the pastel stick toward the back end, and use your thumb and index finger to control the strokes. This grip is ideal for creating fine lines and details. However it offers less control than the other grips.

Broad Strokes Place the pastel flat on the paper and slide it back and forth to create broad linear strokes. This grip is also useful to create a "wash"; use the length of the pastel to cover large areas and create back-grounds quickly.

Round Strokes Turn the pastel stick on its end and grip it toward the front to create short, rounded strokes. This grip is perfect for creating texture quickly in large areas. Try overlapping the rounded strokes to create a denser texture.

Crosshatching *Hatched* strokes are a series of parallel lines; *crosshatched* strokes are simply hatched lines layered over one another, but in opposite directions. You can crosshatch strokes of the same color to create texture or use several different colors to create an interesting blend.

Pointillism Another way to build up color for backgrounds or other large areas of color is to use a series of dots, a technique called "pointillism." This technique creates a rougher, more textured blend. When viewed from a distance, the dots appear to merge, creating one color.

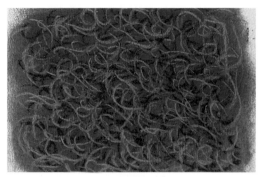

Removing Pigment When you need to remove color from a given area, use a kneaded eraser to pick up the pigment. The more pressure you apply, the more pigment will be removed. Keep stretching and kneading the eraser to expose clean, new surfaces.

Creating Patterns To create textures or patterns when rendering fabric or clothing, first lay down a solid layer of color using the side of the pastel stick or pencil. Then use the point of a pastel pencil to draw a pattern, using several different colors if you wish.

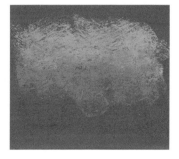

Using Tape You can create straight, even edges by using house painter's tape. Just apply it to your support, and make sure the edges are pressed down securely. Apply the pastel as you desire, and then peel off the tape to reveal the straight edges.

Gradating on a Textured Support Creating a smooth, even gradation on a textured ground can be a little tricky. Add the colors one at a time, applying the length of the stick and letting it skip over the texture of the paper by using light pressure.

Glazing Create a "glaze" just as you might with watercolor by layering one color over another. Use the length of the pastel stick with light pressure to skim over the paper lightly. The result is a new hue—a smooth blend of the two colors.

Blending Pastels

There are a number of ways to blend pastel, and the method you use depends on the effect you want to achieve and the size of the area you're blending. Smooth, even blends are easy to achieve with a brush, a rag, or even your fingers. You can also use your finger or a paper blending stump to soften fine lines and details. Still another method is to place two or more colors next to each other on the support and allow the eye to visually blend them together.

Applying Unblended Strokes In this example, magenta is layered loosely over a yellow background. The strokes are not blended together, and yet from a distance the color appears orange—a mix of the two colors.

Blending with Fingers Using your fingers to blend gives you the softest blend and the most control, but be sure to wipe your hands after each stroke so you don't muddy your work. Or use rubber gloves to keep your hands clean.

Blending with a Tortillon For blending small areas, some artists use a paper blending stump, or *tortillon*. Use the point to soften details and to reach areas that require precise attention.

Creating a Gradation With soft pastel, you can create an even color gradation to depict sunset skies or smooth water. Just start with two spots of color, and then blend the area where they meet.

Masking

The dusty nature of pastel makes it hard to create clean, hard edges; but employing a simple masking technique is a great way to produce sharp edges. To mask, use a piece of paper or tape to create a straight edge (see page 9), or create a clean-edged shape with a special mask you make yourself. Of course, you would use tape only to save the white of the paper; never apply it to a support that already has pigment on it.

Cutting the Shape Begin by drawing the shape on a piece of tracing paper and cutting it out.

Applying the Color After painting the background, place the mask on top and then apply color.

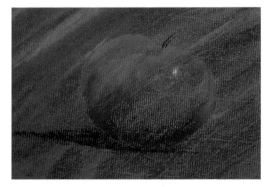

Removing the Mask Carefully peel away the mask to reveal the crisp shape underneath.

Using a Combination of Techniques

All of the techniques mentioned so far are useful in and of themselves, but you won't truly understand the effects you can achieve until you apply them to an actual subject. Here you can see how the same subject is rendered using three different methods; notice the different look each example has. Then practice creating some examples of your own.

Blending Here the colors were applied thickly and smoothly; as you can see, the even layers of color create the appearance of a slick, smooth object.

Linear Strokes In this example, linear strokes are layered over one another to create a more textured appearance. From a distance, the colors still appear to blend together.

Pointillism In this case, pointillism is used to create the form of the sphere. Although the same colors are used, the surface of the object appears much rougher.

The way you approach a painting in pastel is similar to painting in any other medium: Start with an undercolor and then build up the values from dark to light. I begin almost every painting I create (including the landscape shown here) by *toning* the support (applying a base color to cover the "white" of the support) with a wash of acrylic paint. Then I sketch or transfer my drawing to the support and begin blocking in and filling the main shapes. Next I determine the direction and intensity of the light source and begin to define the shapes. Then I work toward harmonizing the colors in the piece, developing the forms and values, and creating interest. Finally I refine the shapes and edges and add the details. When I'm done, it's easy to go back and adjust any areas that need attention by moving or even removing pigment.

Step One I begin by toning a piece of sanded pastel paper with a diluted wash of acrylic paint. Toning assures that none of the unpainted support will show and allows a bit of color to sparkle through subsequent layers of color, harmonizing the finished piece. For the wash, I make a mixture of half yellow ochre paint and half water, and then I brush it evenly over the entire support. (I use an inexpensive brush because the sanded paper will eventually destroy it.) I let the support dry for about 20 minutes, and then I roughly sketch the scene with a pastel pencil, using a color that matches the subject. I start adding color from the top so that the pastel dust falls on the unpainted portion of the support, preventing it from contaminating any areas I've already worked on.

Step Two Next I block in the shapes of the darkest values in the scene, establishing the value relationships throughout the piece. Once I've placed the darks, I can judge the values of the midtones and lights based on how they compare to that darkest value. I always compare the values of the shapes in the subject to those around it; this way, I can determine the darkest darks and the lightest lights. These important contrasts in value create a sense of depth and realism in a painting.

12

Step Three Now I block in the rest of the elements in the scene, building the values from dark to light. I weave in bits of the same colors throughout the piece to unify the color scheme and create a sense of color harmony. I am continually adjusting the forms and values as I work, judging them against one another to make sure they are accurate compared to my reference photo.

Step Four Finally I add the lightest lights—in this case, the highlight on the snow at the end of the pathway—and create the final details. When working with pastel, keep in mind that less is more—you don't want to overwork the piece. One of the most important aspects of painting in pastel is learning to recognize when to stop.

Every good painting begins with a dynamic composition. *Composition* refers not only to the design or layout of a scene, but also to the relationship among the objects in the scene. Whether your subject is a still life or a landscape, the same rules of composition apply: A good composition uses a visual path to lead the viewer's eye in and around the painting, toward the focal point (also called the "center of interest"), which is typically placed off-center. The easiest way to create a visual path in a landscape is to include curving lines that lead from the foreground of the scene toward the focus. Another way to attract the eye is to place bright, warm colors near your focal point. In this example, the curve of the road and the bright yellow trees draw your eye toward the car, which is the center of interest. The dark trees on the right act as a *stopper;* they prevent your eye from wandering away from the focal point and off the page.

Color Palette

SOFT PASTELS: black, burnt umber, cadmium orange, cold medium gray, dark gray-blue, light gray, neutral gray light, olive green, peach, permanent red pale, quinacridone violet, red oxide, rich umber, and white   HARD PASTELS: black, cold light gray, and dark red

Step One Once I have toned my support, I start blocking in the main shapes of the elements in the scene. I use burnt umber in the foreground, cadmium orange for the tree masses, and light gray for the road. I want to allow the color of the paper to show through in the orange trees, so I'm careful not to make the underpainting too thick.

Step Two Next I add red oxide to the middle ground tree shapes and add dark gray-blue and rich umber in the foreground. Then I start to darken the road in the foreground with blue-gray to achieve a clear separation of dark and light—this will create a greater sense of drama in the finished scene.

Step Three Now I use permanent red pale and white for the *negative shapes* in the sky (the spaces between the leaves and the branches of the trees). I want the orange trees to seem airy and lacy, so I alternate between working on the negative shapes in the sky and on the positive shapes in the trees to achieve the illusion of the light sparkling through the leaves. I add black to some of the foreground shapes, as well as to the end of the road, and blend slightly with my finger. I place these darks carefully (and sparingly) to lead the viewer's eye to the focal point of the painting.

Step Four In the foreground and middle ground, I weave in some beautiful, rich fall colors: olive green, quinacridone violet, and red oxide. Here I blend the colors with my finger, taking care not to overblend. I don't want to cover every bit of paper completely—this way, the ground will shimmer through in places, contributing to the color harmony in the piece.

Step Five I use a sharpened black hard pastel stick to indicate the tree trunks and branches. Using the point of the stick to create a thin calligraphic line, I focus on the gesture of the branches rather than on drawing each individual branch that I see. When I'm satisfied with the main branches, I use a dark red hard stick to suggest the branches behind the black ones. Then I use cold medium gray and neutral gray light to draw the car, crimson to indicate the lights, and black to create the window shape. I add the cast shadow of the car on the road to help "anchor" the car to the ground.

6

Step Six At the last moment, I decide to include the telephone pole and wires from the reference photo in my rendering. I use a cold light gray hard stick for the wires, creating a broken line to make it seem as though the wires are shimmering in the light. Then I add peach for the line in shadow. Next I add some variety to the colors in the foreground shadow, including detailing the "white" lines with permanent red deep. I also indicate some falling leaves in the foreground and middle ground with cadmium orange. Then I sign my piece and it's ready for framing.

Setting Up a Still Life

Composing a still life gives you a great deal of control over the subject because all the decisions are up to you! You can choose the lighting, the background, the type of objects you want to include, and what textures you want to depict. Try selecting objects with a variety of shapes and sizes, and be sure to overlap the elements to avoid a stagnant composition. Also keep in mind that it's easier to control an artificial light source rather than relying on natural light—with artificial light, the shadows will remain constant throughout the painting process. Because careful observation is so important in still life painting, I place my setup slightly below eye level, and I stand close to it so I can see the details. For this painting, I tested a number of light sources and arrangements before settling on the most visually interesting setup—a slightly asymmetric arrangement with a strong light source coming from the left.

Color Palette

SOFT PASTELS: burnt umber, fern green, light Naples yellow, light sap green, light turquoise blue, light warm gray, nut brown, viridian green, white, and yellow ochre. HARD PASTELS: carmine, cold deep gray, lemon yellow, light blue, light sap green, light turquoise blue, peacock blue, salmon pink, sanguine, shell pink, and warm medium gray

Step One I set up the elements on several different levels, and I choose objects with a variety of textures and colors to help me create a compelling composition. Then I tone the support with a wash of yellow ochre acrylic. (See page 12.) For the initial drawing, I use a cold deep gray hard pastel that will be easily covered by the subsequent layers of color. I draw the basic shapes of the bowl, the fruit, and the drape, paying particular attention to the ellipse of the bowl. I also outline some of the shadow shapes and the contours of the objects.

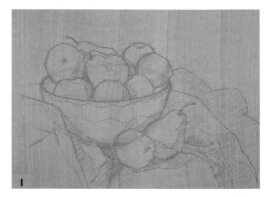

Step Two I continue using hard pastels to block in the basic shapes, working quickly and using the sides of the sticks so I don't fill in the tooth of the paper completely. I cover the background with shell pink, then paint the green apples with light sap green, the lemon with lemon yellow, and the peaches with layers of salmon pink and shell pink. I use light sap green for the green pears and a mix of sanguine and salmon pink for the red pear. For the stripes on the bowl, I apply light turquoise blue in the light areas and peacock blue in the dark areas. I also block in the cast shadow on the wall with warm medium gray. Then I use carmine to add some dark values in between the fruit and on the shadows.

Step Three Next I block in the drape, using shell pink for the light areas, light blue for the shadows on the drape and the wall, and medium warm gray for the shadows on the fruit. Here I use the length of the pastel sticks to apply color, but I don't press very hard; I allow the texture and the color of the toned paper to show through.

Step Four I observe my setup carefully to determine where each piece of fruit has a *form* shadow (a shadow on the object itself that helps to define its shape), a *core* shadow (the darkest part of the form shadow), and a *cast* shadow (a dark shadow that the object throws onto another surface). Some of the cast shadows fall on other pieces of fruit, and some fall on the drape or on the background. But each one follows and reveals the form of the objects they fall on. When I add the core shadow to each piece of fruit, its *reflected light*—the light bouncing off another object onto this one—is also revealed. The reflected light is a lighter value than the core shadow but slightly darker than the highlight. I use fern green for the core shadow of the lemon, and I switch to viridian green for the core shadow and the cast shadow of the green pear.

19

Step Five Once I have the forms of each element worked out, I begin to focus on the nuances of color and value that initially intrigued me in this scene. I add some light sap green to the top of the red pear. Then I layer the background with light Naples yellow in the center, adding light turquoise blue and warm light gray as I work toward the edges. Here I'm actually blending by layering, so I don't use my finger to blend at all. Next I darken the cast shadows against the wall with burnt umber.

Lighting Your Subject

When you're working with a controlled light source, you can experiment with different angles to get various effects. But rather than lighting your subject simply from the front, try establishing your light source to one side and slightly above your subject, as I've done here, to create form and cast shadows that are more distinct.

Contrasting Textures Light reflects off various surfaces differently, which is why it's important to include a variety of surface textures in your setup.

Step Six Now I make some final adjustments to the drape, using a bit of white for the highlights and blending some areas with my finger to soften the transitions. I apply yellow ochre to the center of the bowl, and I add some highlights to the fruit with a mixture of white and light Naples yellow. I also make sure that the highlights on the shiny fruits are more defined than the highlights on the surface of the fuzzy peaches. I create the stems to the fruit with nut brown, and then I add burnt umber on the shadowed side of each stem. Finally I blend the background a bit with my finger to smooth out the strokes.

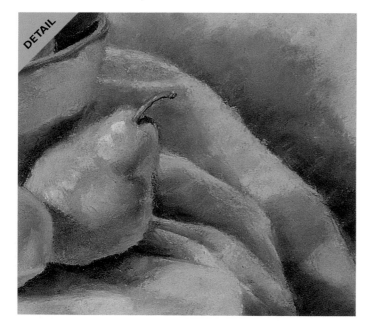

Shadow Detail Cast shadows (such as those the bowl casts on the wall and the pear casts on the drape) have cleaner, harder edges than form shadows—such as the shadows on the pear itself. Form shadows tend to have softer, less dramatic edges, so I take care to blend them smoothly.

Creating Depth

Every landscape painter strives to translate the feeling of a three-dimensional scene onto a flat, two-dimensional surface. But this task becomes more approachable when you understand the basic principles of *atmospheric* or *aerial perspective*. As objects (such as trees or mountains) recede into the distance, the particles in the atmosphere cause them to appear lighter, bluer, and less detailed than the objects in the foreground. In this example, I use these visual cues to depict a sense of depth: I create more detail in the objects in the foreground to make them appear closer, and I use cooler colors in the background and warmer colors in the foreground. Since warm colors appear to come forward in a scene, the oranges and yellows I use in the foreground make the foliage appear closer to the viewer than the distant trees.

Color Palette

SOFT PASTELS: cobalt blue light, cold dark gray, cool middle gray, deep red madder, deep violet, light orange, light violet-blue, moss green, pale yellow, peach warm gray, permanent green, phthalocyanine (phthalo) blue deep, quinacridone violet, turquoise blue, violet, and yellow ochre HARD PASTELS: fern green and spruce blue PASTEL PENCILS: light gray

Step One I often begin with a quick thumbnail sketch on a piece of scrap paper to work out the composition. To help convey a sense of depth in a landscape, it's important to establish a distinctive foreground, middle ground, and background. I also simplify my subject into areas of light, middle, and dark values. Once I've worked out the sketch, I create my final drawing on a piece of sanded pastel paper with a light gray pastel pencil that won't show through in my final painting.

Step Two Once my sketch is complete, I make sure to leave a small border around the edge of the paper to give myself some flexibility in the composition. Then, starting from the top, I begin blocking in the sky with light orange and a bit of violet. I also block in the distant tree line on the horizon with turquoise blue; I want this blue to be a cool base color for the darker blue-green that I will eventually use to cover most of it. These cool colors will help create the illusion that the trees are receding into the distance.

Step Three Next I start establishing some of the middle value shapes on the banks of the river in the middle ground, using moss green, peach warm gray, and cool middle gray. I establish the key shapes, but I know that these will probably change a bit as I go. I also create the larger shapes of the water with light violet-blue. The colors I use here are slightly warmer than those in the background, but they are slightly cooler than those I will use in the foreground.

Step Four I add the darks of the background tree line with a spruce blue hard pastel, pressing firmly to cover most of the turquoise blue undercoat. Using hard pastel for the base coat will allow me to add more layers of soft pastel over it later. I add darks in the water reflections and the foreground water with phthalo blue deep, and I rework some of the water shapes. At this point, I've established most of my complete range of values. I add some darks into the water where the tree line is reflected with cold dark gray. Then I use deep violet to gradate the water in the foreground.

23

5

Step Five I "punch up" the light on the horizon in front of the tree line with pale yellow. Next I add deep red madder into the moss shapes in the middle and foreground, which will make them appear to "pop" forward. This is really the exciting part, where the piece is coming together and begins to take on a life of its own!

6

Step Six I add the details sparingly, creating some calligraphic strokes of quinacridone violet, permanent green, and yellow ochre in the foreground brush to bring it forward even more. To depict the bits of grass floating on the surface of the water, I add short strokes of a fern green hard pastel stick to contrast the dark blue of the water in the foreground. I carefully adjust some of the highlights in the water with cobalt blue light. When I feel I've achieved a sense of depth in the scene, I know my painting is complete.

Using Photo References

With traditional and digital photography, you can work in the studio at any hour and in any season. But there are a few things to keep in mind when working from photos. First you must realize that the camera is not discriminating—it doesn't decide what the most important element is in a scene, so it's your job as an artist to make choices that will make your piece more than merely a copy of a photograph. Experiment with cropping out some elements to simplify a scene, or change the angle of your shot to get a different viewpoint. Also keep in mind that photos tend to distort perspective (especially if you use a wide-angle lens), so you should never trace a photograph. It's best to use your snapshots as starting points, knowing that you can edit the image when you need to. For this painting, I took several shots of the location and then combined them to create the final composition.

Color Palette

SOFT PASTELS: bottle green, burnt umber, dark rose, deep yellow, gray-blue, ivory, light cool gray, light sap green, olive green, palm green, peacock blue, permanent green, phthalo blue, raw sienna, rose madder, rose madder dark, rose madder light, rust, spruce blue, turquoise blue, white, and yellow ochre HARD PASTELS: light cool gray and rust PASTEL PENCILS: light gray

Combining Photos

You can't always capture the scene in just one shot; for this piece, I used a combination of reference photos, picking and choosing the elements I liked from each. In this case, I used the sky from one shot and a close-up of the barn from another. (For more on changing the elements using artistic license, see page 60.)

Step One First I tone a piece of sanded paper with yellow ochre acrylic paint and allow it to dry. Then I sketch the horizon line and the main shapes with a light gray pastel pencil. Next I block in the sky with phthalo blue, leaving the paper blank where I plan to place the large cloud shapes. I block in the undersides of the clouds with gray-blue and use rose madder light on the tops. Then I add some dark rose in the middle of the cloud shapes.

26

Step Two Next I block in the tree line on the horizon with peacock blue, and I rough in the large reddish tree with rust on the light side and rose madder dark on the shadowed side. I also use the length of the rust hard pastel to block in the large shape of the roof, keeping the paper showing where I'll place the pine tree in front. Then I add the shadow to the side of the barn with a mixture of dark rose and turquoise blue, using light pressure so I don't fill the entire tooth of the paper. I paint the light side of the barn with ivory, and then I paint the center pine tree and the bushes at the right of the barn with palm green. I also block in the remaining trees with olive green on the shadow side and light sap green on the highlight side.

Step Three Now I darken the tree line on the horizon with spruce blue, and I rough in the grass around the barn with deep yellow, yellow ochre, and ivory. Then I create the cast shadows of the trees with olive green and turquoise blue. In the foreground, I lay in some palm green, permanent green, and spruce blue, allowing quite a bit of the toned paper to show through.

Step Four I add a variety of color to the red tree with burnt sienna, rose madder deep, and spruce blue. Then I darken the bushes under the two trees on the right. Next I add the cast shadow of the pine tree to the rooftop with rose madder deep, and then I decide to darken the shadowed side of the barn with a light layer of the phthalo blue I used in the sky. I draw in the dark overhang of the rooftop with spruce blue; then I add white to the light sides of the barn and shed, applying the pastel in even, parallel strokes to emulate the siding of the barn. I make sure to stroke up toward the vanishing point. As I add white, I use it as an opportunity to "cut in" and define the negative shapes around the tree in front of the light side of the barn. Then I give the pine tree a shadow side with bottle green.

Step Five Next I add some olive green bushes behind and to the left of the barn. I have to press fairly hard, as there are already several layers of pastel here. I add a few spots of old lilac to the red tree and a few bits of turquoise to the foreground trees. I also add some ivory highlights to the foreground trees.

28

Step Six I complete the foreground trees by adding burnt umber to the dark side of the tree trunks and light cool gray for the light side. Then I add the telephone pole and wires with a sharp, light cool gray hard stick, drawing the wires with broken lines to emulate the way they appear to shimmer in the sunlight. Finally I layer the foreground with more palm green and olive green and indicate some grasses in the foreground shadows with raw sienna.

Using Two-Point Perspective

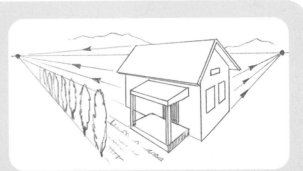

The concept of perspective can be intimidating to some artists, but it's simply a way to represent three dimensions on a flat surface. When an object recedes into the distance, its receding lines seem to converge at a point on the horizon called the "vanishing point." If the lines are on one

Vanishing Points In this example, the two points at each end of the horizon mark the vanishing points. Notice that the elements in the scene get smaller as they approach the vanishing points.

plane, the receding lines converge at one vanishing point; this is referred to as "one-point perspective." But if there are two planes involved, such as a building viewed from a corner, each plane has its own vanishing point, called "two-point perspective." In this example, the corner of the house is closest to us, and the two sides recede toward two different points on the horizon. If you were sketching this scene, you could try placing a straightedge on any line on this house and continue to one of the vanishing points to make sure the perspective is correct.

Depicting Clouds and Skyscapes

Clouds and skies are beautiful and interesting painting subjects, and pastel is perfect for capturing the soft, billowy nature of cloudy skies. With soft pastels, you can convey the transparency of wispy clouds by using less pigment—or you can depict the thick, dark, ominous feel of storm clouds by layering heavy applications of color. Once you've learned to render realistic clouds, you can use them to add a sense of drama in your landscapes. In some cases, the clouds are so intriguing that they become more than just elements in the painting—they become the entire focus! For example, I composed this skyscape based on a photo I took on my way home one evening. The sky was so beautiful and the clouds were so spectacular that I had to pull over and capture it on film. Later I realized if I hadn't taken the photo as proof of this amazing sky, some might think I created the painting from my imagination!

Color Palette

SOFT PASTELS: blue-violet, burnt sienna, burnt umber, cerulean blue light, dark purple-gray, hyacinth violet, ivory, light blue, medium cool gray, permanent red light, phthalo blue deep, quinacridone violet, raw sienna, and ultramarine blue light
HARD PASTELS: red carmine, spruce blue, and violet rouge

Step One First I tone my support with yellow ochre acrylic paint; once it's dry, I lightly sketch the basic shapes of the clouds. Remember that each cloud shape has a form shadow and reflected light. Sometimes it may even be casting a shadow onto another cloud or on the ground, so be sure to observe carefully and then draw all of the shapes you see. Then I draw the rest of the elements in the scene, keeping the horizon line deliberately low to maximize the visual impact of the dramatic sky.

Step Two It's practically impossible to render the complex details of each cloud, so I concentrate on capturing the main shapes, colors, and values. I choose hyacinth violet for the thinner clouds at the upper left, and paint some cerulean blue light breaking through. Then I use permanent red light for the lightest cloud shapes, ultramarine blue light for the clouds nearest the horizon, and phthalo blue deep for the darkest clouds at the top right. I apply the colors with light pressure and stroke across the surface of the paper with the side of the stick.

Step Three Next I work from the top down toward the horizon, adding dark purple-gray at the lower left of the sky and light blue on the right where the blue sky breaks through the clouds. Then I block in the tree line with a red carmine hard stick. This complementary base color will add to the rich color of the trees when I paint over them with green.

Step Four Now I begin to work on the bright clouds just at the horizon, adding ivory and permanent red light. I press hard with the soft sticks to fill the tooth of the paper almost completely. This area is the focal point of the scene—the rest of the cloud shapes and the contrast between the lightest lights and darkest darks will lead the viewer's eye here.

31

Step Five Then I establish the darks in the tree line with hard pastel sticks of spruce blue and violet rouge. At this point I have to use a fair amount of pressure as I'm layering these hard pastel colors over a previous layer of hard pastel. Now you can see how the cool greens I add look so much richer over the red base coat than they would on the plain paper.

Step Six Next I block in the foreground with burnt umber, burnt sienna, and raw sienna. I apply some quinacridone violet in the extreme foreground, weaving it into and skipping it across the other colors with light pressure. I leave some areas of the paper showing through, especially where I plan to indicate the buildings.

Clouds Detail To accurately depict the lacy edges of the clouds, I apply the purple hues I'm using for the sky right next to the cloud shape I want to change. I use the negative space around the cloud (the sky) to "cut" into the positive shape (the cloud) rather than painting over it. This gives me more control over the edges and also creates a smoother transition between the two areas.

Step Seven I go back to the clouds, adjusting some of their shapes to improve the composition. I blend some of the clouds a bit with my finger, filling in some of the areas where there is too much paper showing through. Finally I indicate the buildings with medium cool gray, and then use heavy pressure to add a layer of blue-violet on top.

33

Working with White

When you start to develop an "artist's eye," you'll begin to see the nuances of color in everything around you. For example, at first glance, snow appears white, but if you look more closely, you'll see that it's actually made up of various pastel hues. Like all white objects, snow reflects the colors of the other objects around it—especially the sky. So depending on the time of day, it may appear to be blue, green, pink, or even purple, with pure white only in the brightest highlights. For this piece, I painted the snow with a variety of blues and grays, which help convey the peaceful mood. But I also included some of the brighter hues I used to paint the sky, which makes the scene look more realistic and adds a sense of color harmony to the painting.

Color Palette
SOFT PASTELS: blue, cool gray, dark blue-gray, dark spruce blue, light gray, and light orange-yellow HARD PASTELS: black, red, and spruce blue PASTEL PENCILS: gray

Step One I start by toning my support with a yellow ochre acrylic wash. When my support is dry, I sketch the scene with a gray pastel pencil. Using the side of the pastel sticks, I quickly block in the sky with a gradation (see page 10) of blue and light orange-yellow, leaving some of the paper showing through. For this winter scene, I'll use a limited palette and rely on a lot of pale blues and subtle grays.

Step Two Next I block in the major elements: the background line of trees, the pathway, and the foreground snow. I use cool gray for the pathway and both dark blue-gray and dark spruce blue for the background tree shapes. I paint the middle values of the snow blue. At this point I'm not worried about covering up the sketch of the trees— I can always go back to my reference photo later if I need to. But I make sure that I don't apply too much pigment at this early stage.

Step Three Now I add a layer of light gray in the foreground and highlight the snow with some of the same light orange-yellow I used in the sky. This helps to harmonize the piece and gives the snow some sparkle. It also leads the viewer's eye in toward the end of the pathway, which is my focal point. To give the snow a soft quality, I blend it a bit with my finger.

Step Four I go back to my reference photo to render the trees, but I keep in mind that I don't need to draw each individual branch. I place the main trunks with a black hard pastel, and then I draw the secondary branches with a hard spruce blue hard stick. Next I switch to a red hard pastel to render some of the tiny branches at the top of the tree.

Tree Branch Detail

To make my trees look realistic, I make sure to creates strokes that are thicker at the top and taper slightly as they extend out and up.

Step Five Now I add the finishing touches. I give each tree a cast shadow with gray-blue, and I decide to include some simple footprints in the snow for interest. Because this isn't in my reference photo, I need to keep the light source in mind as I create the prints and their shadows. Notice that throughout this piece, I never used white!

Footprints Detail To create the footprints in the snow, I use blue-gray to fill in the shapes. As I place the shapes, I try to create a realistic pattern that will mimic a person's stride. Then I add an orange-yellow highlight on the front edge of each print to indicate where the snow would be higher.

Flowers are timeless and attractive subjects for a painting, and they offer a variety of shapes, colors, and textures to capture on paper. And rendering a floral bouquet gives you the chance to combine various types of flowers and foliage. Although it's probably more convenient to paint from photos, I prefer to paint floral bouquets from life. That way, I can play around with different arrangements before I settle on the one I like best. When I'm setting up a bouquet, I try to create a well-balanced color scheme; for this painting, I chose flowers with complementary colors: purple lilacs and yellow roses.

Color Palette

SOFT PASTELS: burnt umber, cold medium gray, cool gray, fern green, gray phthalo blue-green, light blue, light gray-green, neutral gray-green, palm green, peach, shell pink, spruce blue, Van Dyke brown, warm light gray, warm ochre, white, and yellow ochre light HARD PASTELS: blue-violet, hyacinth violet, light ochre, lilac, and rust PASTEL PENCILS: light gray

Step One For this piece, I choose a piece of white sanded pastel paper that will allow me to see my detailed drawing more clearly. First I create a careful line drawing of the basic shapes with a light gray pastel pencil. I concentrate on the largest flower shapes and think of the daisies as concave disks, facing some toward the light and placing others in shadow. I'm working from life, so I have to work fairly quickly before the flowers start to wilt or droop.

Step Two I use a lilac hard pastel for the middle tones of the lilacs and a hyacinth violet hard pastel for the darks. Then I block in the roses with a light ochre hard pastel, using medium pressure. I use fern green for the eucalyptus leaves in the light and palm green for those in shadow. I place the shadows on the daisies with warm light gray, but I leave the white of the paper showing for the light areas. The centers of the daisies are the same light ochre I use for the roses.

Step Three Next I block in the background with spruce blue, burnt umber, cold medium gray, and palm green. Then I rough in the foreground with shell pink. I use neutral gray green inside the vase and palm green for the stems in the vase. I purposely let some of the paper show through around the edge of the vase where the glass is the thickest, letting the white paper act as the highlight.

Step Four Next I use spruce blue to draw the contours around the leaf shapes and "cut" into the lighter values to define them. I create some texture in the lilacs by using the square end of a blue-violet hard pastel to render the petals. Then I add a layer of light blue in the same manner. I create shadows in the roses with gray phthalo blue-green and I add the edge of the table with cold medium gray. Then I create some stems throughout the arrangement with palm green, adding more in the vase with rust.

Step Five I blend in some Van Dyke brown on the right side of the vase to soften it and add some black to the background. I continue to refine the shapes of the leaves, and I add some more leaves with light blue and light gray-green. Then I focus on the daisies; I want to capture each flower without using too much detail, so I keep my strokes loose. I add peach to the shadowed sides of the daisies, and then I add a little white to the light sides, beginning to cover up the paper.

Step Six Notice that each flower has a light side, a shadowed side, a core shadow, and reflected light. In some instances this is obvious, but in others it's more obscure. To define the roses, I use yellow ochre light to cut into the shapes, and I use light gray-green to depict the reflected light on them. Then I start to give the lilacs more texture, using the same colors as before but making a more concerted effort to shape them by pressing harder and using a variety of strokes.

Step Seven Next I add warm ochre to the inside of the roses and continue to define the leaves and flower shapes. I add more texture to the lilacs, making the lilac on the table a little more solid by creating a dramatic contrast between the light and shadow.

Step Eight In this final stage I add some wispy branches on the eucalyptus with a sharpened rust pastel. I also add Van Dyke brown and cool gray to the vase, blending it smoothly with my finger. I take a step back and assess my work. Once I'm satisfied, I sign my name and the painting is finished!

Conveying Light and Shadow

Although you can't literally create light in a painting, you can create the illusion of light and shadow through the effective use of color and value. When you look at your subject, try to determine the main shapes and colors of the light areas—and keep in mind that the direction and intensity of the light directly influence the colors and shadows in a scene. For example, light coming from behind the subject flattens the forms and illuminates their edges, sometimes creating a halo effect. Side lighting creates strong shadows and highlights, making the forms appear three-dimensional. And when light strikes the subject head-on, the shadows are minimal and the colors are more intense. In this example, the light source is coming from the upper left, causing the warm light to filter through the trees and creating long, cool shadows on the sidewalk.

Color Palette

SOFT PASTELS: black, burnt sienna, cobalt blue-green, cold light gray, cold medium gray, gray-blue, ivory, orange ochre, permanent orange, permanent yellow, permanent yellow deep, permanent yellow lemon, permanent yellow light, raw umber, spruce green, turquoise blue, Van Dyke brown, walnut brown, warm olive green, white, and yellow ochre light
HARD PASTELS: black, burnt sienna, and cold deep gray

Capturing Light I love walking under a canopy of colorful leaves on an autumn afternoon; it's almost as though the light is coming from within the mass of trees. This is because the sunlight is filtering through the almost transparent leaves at an angle. The low viewpoint makes it seem as if we are looking slightly up at the trees, so they appear to be glowing with light.

Step One I begin by toning my paper with yellow ochre acrylic paint and creating my sketch with a cold deep gray hard pastel stick. I draw all the main elements and decide to place the two main tree trunks in the center of the composition. Normally I would avoid placing the focal point in the center of the painting, but in this case the path leads the eye away from the center, so I think it works well.

Step Two Next I start blocking in the main shapes of color, and adding orange ochre to the underside of the foliage. I also use this color to indicate the cast shadows of the trees on the ground. Then I add cold medium gray to block in the foliage in the background and gray-blue to start blocking in the path. I also suggest the shadow across the pathway with cold medium gray. Then I use permanent yellow light to begin building up the color in the foliage and the ground next to the path.

Step Three The contrast between dark and light is important in this piece, so I constantly adjust the values as I work. I darken the foliage behind the trees with spruce green. Then I use a burnt sienna hard pastel to darken the main tree trunks, being careful not to use a solid line so there is room in front of the trunk for the leaves. I add the road behind the trees and some highlights in the foliage with cold light gray, and layer the light areas on the path with blue-gray.

Step Four I use permanent yellow light, permanent yellow lemon, and permanent yellow deep to render the sunlit foliage, and indicate the shadowed shapes underneath with orange ochre and warm olive green. I also make sure to use some of the grays and blues from the path in the leaves. I add black under the foliage, in the background, and on the leading edge of the path on the right. Then I blend walnut brown in with the black, using my finger. I also layer black on the dark sides of the tree trunks to heighten the contrast between the dark trees and the light shapes in the background.

Step Five I continue to refine and adjust the color in the foliage, weaving more layers of permanent yellow and yellow ochre light into the leaves in the foreground. I use small, short strokes and dab with the end of my pastel sticks, pressing fairly hard to cover the layers I've already built up. I add some strokes of burnt sienna, raw umber, and ivory on the pathway to indicate fallen leaves. I lighten the foliage with permanent orange and then blend a few areas lightly with my fingers, but I'm careful not to overblend. Then I add a spot of cobalt blue-green to the end of the path, which helps to lead the viewer's eye down the road.

44

Tree Detail I want to create the appearance of soft light filtering through the leaves, so I allow bits of paper to show through as I work.

Step Six Next I add thin branches with a sharpened black hard pastel, using broken lines to emulate the branches going in and out of the foliage. I also use a burnt sienna hard pastel to add some lighter branches. Then I add dabs of permanent yellow across the tree trunks and the path to indicate falling leaves, and I add a few more strokes of white to represent the light coming through the foliage. I apply turquoise blue on the path and darken the right corner with black and a bit of Van Dyke brown. Then I blend a few spots along the path with my finger, merging the gray and the black a bit more.

Animals have always been a favorite subject for artists, and pastels are ideal for rendering them. With pastels, you can create soft, fluffy fur using smooth blends or depict coarse, wiry hair using fine strokes of pastel pencil; you can even use a paper blending stump to drag and blend one color into another, creating the appearance of a more textured fur. But it's not just the tools and techniques that make an animal rendering realistic—the support you select is also important. Sanded paper makes an excellent support for animal paintings because its rough grain helps convey a tactile texture. But smoother papers also work well, as they can accommodate more layers of color, which is useful for depicting animals with thick fur. For this rendering of a fox, I chose a smooth, middle-toned paper, which provided a good base color for my subject.

Color Palette

SOFT PASTELS: lt. ultramarine blue HARD PASTELS: lt. blue and Van Dyke brown PASTEL PENCILS: black, burnt carmine, burnt umber, caput mortuum, cobalt blue, cold gray, cream, dark indigo, dark umber, dark sepia, lt. flesh, lt. ultramarine blue, lt. yellow ochre, Payne's gray, raw umber, sanguine, terra cotta, turquoise blue, walnut brown, warm gray, white, and yellow ochre

Step One I want to put the fox in a natural environment, so I create a simple background with a tree line and mountains in the distance, using a photo reference for the fox. I begin with a contour drawing of the fox and the main elements in the scene, using a Van Dyke brown hard pastel on the smooth side of a piece of raw sienna paper.

Step Two To help achieve the fine details of the fox's fur and features, I decide to use pastel pencils for the rest of this piece. First I use cobalt blue for the sky and turquoise blue for the wispy clouds and the glow on the horizon. I block in the mountains with caput mortuum and warm gray, and then I use a light flesh stick for the highlight side of the snow and light ultramarine for the shadowed side. Next I use burnt carmine for the base color along the tree line, but I leave the paper showing where I will place the trees above the fox's head. Using the side of the pastel pencil, I start to block in the background snow with light ultra-marine blue and cobalt blue.

Step Three I continue building up values in the snow, and then I begin blocking in the fox's fur with sanguine for the darker areas and terra cotta for the lighter shapes, still using the side of the pencils. In this case, the texture of the paper will help me achieve the softness that I'm looking for. Then I darken the tree line with dark indigo, using heavy pressure to cover most of the red.

Step Four Next I add burnt umber and dark sepia on the tail, and place burnt umber shadows behind the tail and in the ears. For the ears, I draw the negative shapes around the hairs to define them. I use medium pressure and the side of my burnt umber pastel pencil to give more form to the face, darkening the areas between the ears and eyes. I also use burnt umber for the darks around the eyes, and I apply raw umber and terra cotta to the irises. I use warm gray and a bit of white for the area under the eyes and around the nose. Then I fill in the nose with Payne's gray and add a cold gray highlight. Next I fill in the foreground snow with cobalt blue and light ultramarine blue, and I use the point of my Van Dyke brown pencil to draw the tree trunks above the fox's head. I also use dark umber to indicate the bark showing through the snow at the bottom of the support.

Step Six Next I darken the shapes around the eyes and the pupils with the point of a black pastel pencil. I press firmly, filling the tooth of the paper completely. Then I pick out a few highlights in the tail using the point of a yellow ochre pencil. I switch to a light blue hard pastel to define some interesting shapes in the snow, and then I apply a light ultramarine blue soft pastel for the highlights, blending slightly with my finger.

Step Five Next I start to create some highlights in the fur. I use light yellow ochre to draw a few individual hairs in some carefully chosen spots— above the eyes, on the snout, and below the ears. Then I switch to a cream pastel pencil to draw a few hairs on the inside of the ears, using the point of the pencil to make fine strokes. When the point of my pencil gets dull, I sharpen it with an electric sharpener.

Step Seven I add the stars in the night sky with a sharp white pencil, pressing firmly and choosing the placement of each star carefully so they look natural. Then I add white highlights in the fox's eyes and on the nose. I draw a few whiskers with Payne's gray and decide to create some grasses poking through the snow with Van Dyke brown and walnut brown. To finish, I give the grasses in the light subtle cast shadow with cobalt blue.

Using Pastel Pencils

Pastel pencils are somewhat harder than soft pastels sticks, but (depending on the manufacturer) they may also be slightly softer than hard pastel sticks. Because they can be sharpened to a point, pastel pencils can create finer lines than other types of pastel. They are ideal for detail work and crosshatching, but you can also use the side of the pencil to shade and fill in large areas, as shown here. Apply more pressure and make your strokes closer together for dense coverage, and lighten the pressure and loosen the stroke for more sparse coverage.

Painting a Self-Portrait

Artists have been painting portraits in pastel for centuries, perhaps because people are such interesting subjects. But not all artists have the luxury of having a model to pose for them, and sometimes painting yourself is the best way to practice rendering features, skin tones, and proportions. At least you're painting what you know! Creating a self-portrait will give you the opportunity to experiment as much as you like with various poses, angles, lighting, and expressions. Try to paint what you *really see* and not what you *think* you look like. You may find, as I did when painting this self-portrait, that you learn something new about yourself.

Color Palette

SOFT PASTELS: alizarin crimson, carmine, crimson red, light gray, medium neutral gray, permanent red light, raw umber, rust, Van Dyke brown, warm light gray, and white   HARD PASTELS: cocoa brown, coral, flesh pink, ivory, light blue, olive green, peach, rust, sandalwood, sepia, and Van Dyke brown   PASTEL PENCILS: Indian red

Working From a Photo Some artists prefer using a mirror to paint self-portraits from life, but I like working from photos. In this case, I asked my husband to take several photos of me from different angles and positions. Then I studied the photos to determine the correct proportions and main shapes of my face.

Step One I begin by sketching the head on a piece of steel gray paper with an Indian red pastel pencil. First I position the top of the head on the page, and then I place the bottom of the head and determine the width. I divide the head roughly in half horizontally, through the middle of the eyes; then I divide the lower portion of the head into two equal sections, from the middle of the eyes to the bottom of the nose and from the bottom of the nose to the bottom of the chin. I look to make sure that this is consistent with the proportions in my photo. I also divide the head vertically through the bridge of the nose. Using this foundation, I draw the hair shape, the eyes, nose, mouth, ears, and shoulder area. I also look at the drawing in a mirror before moving on; any inconsistencies are more obvious in a mirror image.

50

Step Two Next I establish the darkest values with a Van Dyke brown hard pastel. I use the length of the pastel stick using a light touch, letting the paper show through underneath. This way I can save my midtones and I won't saturate the paper at this point.

Step Three Then I block in the mid-value shadow areas with a sandalwood hard pastel. I use a coral hard pastel to add some initial color to the lips, and I begin to define the hair with cocoa brown. I start with the darker areas and work gradually lighter as I get closer to the light source. It's best to work in the middle and dark values for as long as possible in a portrait, as the lights and whites can look chalky if they are applied too soon.

Step Four I begin to build up the darks in the shadows, using rust for the warm areas and olive for the cool areas. I'm still using hard pastel sticks and blending by layering the color. Next I add some midtones to the side of the face with flesh pink. I use a light touch and leave some of the middle value of the paper showing at the edges of the darks.

Step Five Next I begin slowly building up the skin tones with even pressure. I use raw umber under the mouth and at the core of the neck. I add some alizarin crimson where the cheek is in shadow, and then I create the eyes with layers of light blue hard pastel and olive green. I use peach and ivory hard pastels to build up the light side of the face, keeping the planes of the face in mind. I also add the red shirt, using rust for the main shapes in shadow and a combination of crimson red and permanent red light for the light shapes. I apply these colors in broad strokes, using medium pressure on the length of the pastel and letting the paper show through underneath. I also create some strokes in the background with light gray.

Step Six Next I add some reflected light under the lips with warm light gray, washing it over the small area carefully with very light pressure. Then I start to refine the hair by adding medium neutral gray highlights. I indicate a few individual strands, and then I use Van Dyke brown to darken the shadows in the hair and the eyebrows. I use the tip of the pastel stick to place the eyelashes with the same color. Then I place the shadow of the earring with a sepia hard pastel and the stone in the center with carmine.

Step Seven I continue to refine the shapes of the hair, and then I add white highlights to the eyes. I create the highlights on the lips with flesh pink and blend the skin tones a bit with my fingers. Finally I add some more light gray to the background and blend it into the previous layer with my fingers. When I step back to assess my work, I try to objectively compare the photo with the finished piece to make sure I've achieved a good likeness.

Expressing a Theme

Sometimes using the same subject, color scheme, or style in series of paintings can be a wonderful way to find a focus in your work. Whether you want to make a bold artistic statement or simply capture a specific mood in a body of work, expressing a theme is a great way to expand yourself creatively. It can also help you develop your own style: When you determine a cohesive idea for a group of paintings, you'll start to discover the characteristics that distinguish your work, such as a tendency to paint loosely or a preference for a particular group of colors. Your theme can be as simple as summer gardens, figures, or animals in the wild. I recently decided to develop a group of paintings featuring different women in everyday settings. I chose to begin with a painting of a woman reading at home, and since reading is one of my favorite pastimes, I decided to make it a self-portrait. And because part of creating a theme is determining a style or approach, I chose to use bright colors and a more illustrative style to give these paintings an upbeat, contemporary feel.

Color Palette

HARD PASTELS: light gray PASTEL PENCILS: black, burnt carmine, burnt umber, caput mortuum, cobalt blue, deep ochre, deep purple, earth green, Indian red, indigo blue, lemon yellow, light chrome yellow, light flesh, light turquoise green, light ultramarine blue, manganese violet, medium flesh, medium green, permanent green olive, pine green, pink carmine, raw umber, sanguine, terra cotta, turquoise blue, Van Dyke brown, violet, and white

Step One I begin by sketching out my idea several times until I have what I want. Then I enlarge the sketch on a copy machine. I want to add a pattern to the skirt, so I work out the floral pattern on a separate piece of tissue paper and tape it over the photocopy of the sketch with transparent tape. Then I create a color sketch, using markers to work out my color scheme.

Step Two Next I tone a piece of sanded paper with cadmium red light acrylic paint. While that dries (about 20 minutes), I rub the back of the photocopy with a light gray hard pastel, covering the entire sheet to create a carbon. When the red paper is dry, I tape the copy to it at the top, carbon-side down. Then I use a sharp graphite pencil to trace over the lines to transfer the sketch to the support.

Step Three This painting is small (only about 8" × 10"), and it has quite a bit of detail, so I decide to use only pastel pencils for this piece. While working, I place a clean sheet of tracing paper under my hand so I won't smudge my piece. I start in the upper left with the curtain, using turquoise blue for the darks and light turquoise green for the lights. I press firmly, using the tip of the pastel pencil and blending the two colors together where the edges meet. I use manganese violet for the night sky, earth green for the building on the left, and pink carmine for the other building, and I leave the paper showing in the windows.

Step Four I fill in the pillow with permanent green olive and medium green, and I use Van Dyke brown for the hair. Then I color the shadowed shapes of the face, arms, and legs with caput mortuum. I leave a bit of the red paper showing around all the shapes to create an outline by not filling the shapes in completely. Later I will go back and create a more noticeable outline.

Step Five Next I use violet and manganese violet for the shirt, the ledge, and the coffee cup. Then I fill in the table with terra cotta and use a mix of burnt carmine and pink carmine for the couch. I fill in the dark areas on the dog with deep purple and black, blending the two colors slightly in some areas. Then I create the dog's lighter areas with light turquoise green and light ultramarine blue. I add medium flesh for the lights on the skin, and I place the darks in the hair with burnt umber. Next I fill in the pattern on the skirt with pine green and terra cotta, letting the color of the paper serve for the red lines in the pattern.

Step Six I place some highlights on the skin with light flesh, pressing firmly to cover the previous layers of color. Then I create the red mouth, using pink carmine for the lower lip and burnt carmine for the upper lip in shadow. Next I add the lights in the windows of the background buildings with light chrome yellow. At this point, I've filled in all my dark areas and mid-tones; next I'll focus on adding the lighter areas and the details.

Step Seven Once all the shapes are filled in, I begin to outline the forms with a variety of colors. Sometimes I choose contrasting colors rather than similar ones to create variety and interest. For instance, here I use indigo blue around the left side of the pillow and Indian red around the right side. Then I add sanguine to the skin and draw the eyes, using cobalt blue for the iris and light ultramarine for the whites. I add the eyebrows with burnt umber, and then I indicate the earring, using burnt carmine for the teardrop-shaped bead and raw umber for the gold. I also add small, light strokes of light turquoise green for a highlight on the edge of the skirt.

Step Eight For more interest, I decide to add a swirling texture to all the shapes except the skin areas. I apply the texture on the curtain with cobalt blue, pink carmine, and light turquoise green. For the pillow, I use light turquoise green and pine green. Then I add texture to the dog with cobalt blue and olive green. For the light areas of the couch, I use lemon yellow and pink carmine; for the areas in shadow, I use pink carmine and cobalt blue. I also complete the detail on the dog, adding the highlights in her eyes with deep ochre and white. Finally I add the steam from the coffee cup with light ultramarine and white, pressing firmly to cover the layers underneath.

Taking Artistic License

Once you've mastered the fundamentals of value, color, and composition, you can begin to take liberties with your subject matter. When an artist alters a subject by changing the viewpoint, adding or removing an element from the scene, or enhancing the color scheme, it's called "using artistic license." As you become more comfortable with altering your subject, you may want to take artistic license a step further and try creating a scene entirely from your own imagination— in other words, exercise artistic license with reality in general. In this painting, I began with an image from a dream I'd had and then experimented with various shapes, colors, values, perspectives, and lighting in small thumbnail sketches until I settled on one that appealed to me. To convey the feeling of awe and wonder in the image, I chose to use simple, distorted shapes and bright, unrealistic colors, which lend a surreal quality to the scene.

Color Palette

HARD PASTELS: light gray PASTEL PENCILS: alizarin crimson, black, bright olive green, cadmium red light, cadmium yellow, cobalt blue light, dark blue-green, dark violet, deep yellow, light ultramarine blue, magenta, permanent green deep, permanent rose deep, ultramarine blue, and white

Step One After working out the composition and color scheme of my idea with a few quick thumbnail sketches, I tone a piece of sanded pastel paper with a cadmium red light acrylic wash and let it dry for about 20 minutes. Then I carefully transfer my final drawing to the support with a light gray hard pastel.

Step Two For this piece, I decide to use pastel pencils, which will let me achieve the fine detail I need. I start with black, ultramarine blue, and dark violet for the sky. Then I fill in the snowy hills with cobalt blue light and dark violet, starting with the hill in the background and moving toward those in the foreground.

Step Three Next I work on the distant building, using cadmium red light for the front of the building and magenta for the side. Then I use dark violet to achieve a slight gradation on the side of the building, which tones down the colors of the buildings a bit and allows the main focus to be on the figure. I blend the pigments as I work, pressing each color into the others around it. Then I fill in the windows with dark violet and black layered over one another. I also fill in the foreground building with bright olive green, pressing firmly to fill in the area thoroughly and evenly.

Step Four Next I use permanent green deep for a gradation on the face of the green building. Then I fill in the dark windows with ultramarine blue and black. I outline the windows with permanent rose deep, and then I use deep yellow, cadmium yellow, and white to fill in the brightly lit window. I apply cadmium yellow to the entire path, the doorway, and the doorjamb, leaving the paper blank where the figure will be. I don't butt the cadmium yellow up to the edge of the green building; instead I leave a tiny red outline around the door. Then I add deep yellow to the doorjamb, using white for the highlight at the bottom. I also use deep yellow to indicate the edge of the path at the right.

Step Five Next I carefully remove any remaining marks from the transferred drawing with a rubber eraser. Then I use black to draw the lower tree branches and ultramarine light to draw the upper branches. I fill in the entire shape of the figure with dark blue-green, and I use alizarin crimson to indicate reflected light on the shadow side of her shape. Next I add cadmium yellow to the light side and create the figure's cast shadow, adding alizarin crimson and dark blue-green where her body meets her shadow.

Step Six Now I draw the snowflakes using small strokes of light ultramarine blue, ultramarine blue, permanent green deep, and cadmium yellow, pressing firmly to make sure they are visible. I make smaller strokes to create more distant flakes, as well as larger strokes to indicate closer ones. The strokes are slightly curved to show that the snowflakes are floating gently downward. Then I sign my name!

Conclusion

No matter what subject you choose to explore in your artwork, the more you practice and experiment with pastel, the more you'll discover about the amazing results you can achieve. Keep your camera and sketchbook ready, because whatever captures your interest or your imagination is what will bring style and individuality to your work. Try working with different techniques and materials to find what works best for you, but most important—just keep painting. Use your imagination and enjoy working with pastel!